# BALLAD
## PLAYALONG SOLOS FOR ALTO SAX

| | PAGE NUMBER | CD TRACK NUMBER |
|---|---|---|
| Bridge Over Troubled Water | 2 | 1 |
| Bring Him Home | 4 | 2 |
| I Dreamed a Dream | 5 | 3 |
| Candle in the Wind | 6 | 4 |
| Don't Cry for Me Argentina | 8 | 5 |
| I Don't Know How to Love Him | 10 | 6 |
| I Know Him So Well | 12 | 7 |
| Imagine | 14 | 8 |
| Killing Me Softly with His Song | 16 | 9 |
| Nights in White Satin | 18 | 10 |
| One Day I'll Fly Away | 20 | 11 |
| Wonderful Tonight | 22 | 12 |
| B♭ *Tuning Notes* | | 13 |
| *A Tuning Notes* | | 14 |

Arrangements by Jack Long

## HOW TO USE THE CD ACCOMPANIMENT:

A melody cue appears on the right channel only. If your CD player has a balance adjustment, you can adjust the volume of the melody by turning down the right channel.

ISBN 978-0-634-00450-6

HAL•LEONARD®
CORPORATION
7777 W. BLUEMOUND RD. P.O. BOX 13819 MILWAUKEE, WI 53213

Visit Hal Leonard Online at
**www.halleonard.com**

# BRIDGE OVER TROUBLED WATER ◆❶

Words and Music by
PAUL SIMON

ALTO SAX

# BRING HIM HOME
from LES MISÉRABLES

Music by CLAUDE-MICHEL SCHÖNBERG
Lyrics by HERBERT KRETZMER and ALAIN BOUBLIL

ALTO SAX

# I DREAMED A DREAM ❸

from LES MISÉRABLES

Music by CLAUDE-MICHEL SCHÖNBERG
Lyrics by HERBERT KRETZMER
Original Text by ALAIN BOUBLIL and JEAN-MARC NATEL

ALTO SAX

# CANDLE IN THE WIND

Music by ELTON JOHN
Words by BERNIE TAUPIN

ALTO SAX

# DON'T CRY FOR ME ARGENTINA ♦5

from EVITA

Words by TIM RICE
Music by ANDREW LLOYD WEBBER

ALTO SAX

MCA MUSIC PUBLISHING

# I DON'T KNOW HOW TO LOVE HIM 6
from JESUS CHRIST SUPERSTAR

Words by TIM RICE
Music by ANDREW LLOYD WEBBER

Alto Sax

# I KNOW HIM SO WELL
from CHESS

Words and Music by BENNY ANDERSSON,
TIM RICE and BJORN ULVAEUS

ALTO SAX

# IMAGINE ◆8

14

Words and Music by
JOHN LENNON

ALTO SAX

rall.

# KILLING ME SOFTLY WITH HIS SONG

Words by NORMAN GIMBEL
Music by CHARLES FOX

ALTO SAX

# NIGHTS IN WHITE SATIN ◆10◆

Words and Music by
JUSTIN HAYWOOD

ALTO SAX

# ONE DAY I'LL FLY AWAY  ⑪

Words and Music by
JOE SAMPLE and WILL JENNINGS

ALTO SAX

MCA MUSIC PUBLISHING

# WONDERFUL TONIGHT

Words and Music by
ERIC CLAPTON

ALTO SAX

# PLAY MORE OF YOUR FAVORITE SONGS
## WITH GREAT INSTRUMENTAL FOLIOS FROM HAL LEONARD

### Best of the Beatles
89 of the greatest songs from the legends of Liverpool, including: All You Need Is Love • And I Love Her • The Fool on the Hill • Got to Get You into My Life • Here, There, and Everywhere • Let It Be • Norwegian Wood • Something • Ticket to Ride • and more.

| | | |
|---|---|---|
| 00847217 | Flute | $9.95 |
| 00847218 | Clarinet | $9.95 |
| 00847219 | Alto Sax | $9.95 |
| 00847220 | Trumpet | $9.95 |
| 00847221 | Trombone | $9.95 |

### The Definitive Jazz Collection
88 songs, including: Ain't Misbehavin' • All the Things You Are • Birdland • Body and Soul • A Foggy Day • Girl From Ipanema • Love for Sale • Mercy, Mercy, Mercy • Moonlight in Vermont • Night and Day • Skylark • Stormy Weather • and more.

| | | |
|---|---|---|
| 08721673 | Flute | $9.95 |
| 08721674 | Clarinet | $9.95 |
| 08721675 | Alto Sax | $9.95 |
| 08721676 | Trumpet | $9.95 |
| 08721677 | Trombone | $9.95 |

### Broadway Showstoppers
47 incredible selections from over 25 shows. Songs include: All I Ask of You • Cabaret • Camelot • Climb Ev'ry Mountain • Comedy Tonight • Don't Cry for Me Argentina • Hello, Dolly! • I Dreamed a Dream • Maria • Memory • Oklahoma! • Seventy-Six Trombones • and many more!

| | | |
|---|---|---|
| 08721339 | Flute | $6.95 |
| 08721340 | B♭ Clarinet | $6.95 |
| 08721341 | E♭ Alto Sax | $6.95 |
| 08721342 | B♭ Trumpet/B♭ Tenor Sax | $6.95 |
| 08721343 | Trombone (Bass Clef Instruments) | $6.95 |

### Definitive Rock 'n' Roll Collection
95 classics, including: Barbara Ann • Blue Suede Shoes • Blueberry Hill • Duke of Earl • Earth Angel • Gloria • The Lion Sleeps Tonight • Louie, Louie • My Boyfriend's Back • Rock Around the Clock • Stand by Me • The Twist • Wild Thing • and more!

| | | |
|---|---|---|
| 00847207 | Flute | $9.95 |
| 00847208 | Clarinet | $9.95 |
| 00847209 | Alto Sax | $9.95 |
| 00847210 | Trumpet | $9.95 |
| 00847211 | Trombone | $9.95 |

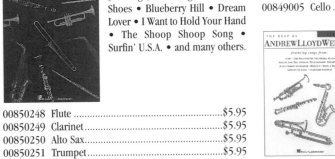

### Choice Jazz Standards
30 songs, including: All the Things You Are • A Foggy Day • The Girl From Ipanema • Just in Time • My Funny Valentine • Quiet Nights of Quiet Stars • Smoke Gets in Your Eyes • Watch What Happens • and many more.

| | | |
|---|---|---|
| 00850276 | Flute | $5.95 |
| 00850275 | Clarinet | $5.95 |
| 00850274 | Alto Sax | $5.95 |
| 00850273 | Trumpet | $5.95 |
| 00850272 | Trombone | $5.95 |

### Disney's The Lion King
5 fun solos for students from Disney's blockbuster. Includes: Can You Feel the Love Tonight • Circle of Life • Hakuna Matata • I Just Can't Wait to Be King • Be Prepared.

| | | |
|---|---|---|
| 00849949 | Flute | $5.95 |
| 00849950 | Clarinet | $5.95 |
| 00849951 | Alto Sax | $5.95 |
| 00849952 | Trumpet | $5.95 |
| 00849953 | Trombone | $5.95 |
| 00849955 | Piano Accompaniment | $9.95 |
| 00849003 | Easy Violin | $5.95 |
| 00849004 | Viola | $5.95 |
| 00849005 | Cello | $5.95 |

### Classic Rock & Roll
31 songs, including: Blue Suede Shoes • Blueberry Hill • Dream Lover • I Want to Hold Your Hand • The Shoop Shoop Song • Surfin' U.S.A. • and many others.

| | | |
|---|---|---|
| 00850248 | Flute | $5.95 |
| 00850249 | Clarinet | $5.95 |
| 00850250 | Alto Sax | $5.95 |
| 00850251 | Trumpet | $5.95 |
| 00850252 | Trombone | $5.95 |

### Best of Andrew Lloyd Webber
26 of his best, including: All I Ask of You • Close Every Door • Don't Cry for Me Argentina • I Don't Know How to Love Him • Love Changes Everything • Memory • and more.

| | | |
|---|---|---|
| 00849939 | Flute | $6.95 |
| 00849940 | Clarinet | $6.95 |
| 00849941 | Trumpet | $6.95 |
| 00849942 | Alto Sax | $6.95 |
| 00849943 | Trombone | $6.95 |
| 00849015 | Violin | $6.95 |

FOR MORE INFORMATION, SEE YOUR LOCAL MUSIC DEALER, OR WRITE TO:

**HAL•LEONARD CORPORATION**
7777 W. BLUEMOUND RD. P.O. BOX 13819 MILWAUKEE, WI 53213

Prices, contents, and availability subject to change without notice.
Disney characters and artwork © The Walt Disney Company.

0299